Cambridge English Readers

···

Level 2

Series editor: Philip Prowse

One Day

Helen Naylor

CAMBRIDGE
UNIVERSITY PRESS

CAMBRIDGE
UNIVERSITY PRESS

University Printing House, Cambridge CB2 8BS, United Kingdom

Cambridge University Press is part of the University of Cambridge.

It furthers the University's mission by disseminating knowledge in the pursuit of education, learning and research at the highest international levels of excellence.

www.cambridge.org
Information on this title: www.cambridge.org/9780521714228

First published 2008
Reprinted 2016

Helen Naylor has asserted her right to be identified as the Author of the Work in accordance with the Copyright, Design and Patents Act 1988.

Printed in the United Kingdom by Hobbs the Printers Ltd

Illustrations by Kathryn Baker

A catalogue record of this publication is available from the British Library.

ISBN 978-0-521-71422-8 Paperback

Contents

People in the story

Jason: a seventeen-year-old boy; lives with his mother at 12, Moreland Road in Bath
Maria: Jason's girlfriend
Nina Sen: lives at 48, Moreland Road; works in a bank
David Sen: Nina's husband; works as the top cook in a French restaurant
Max: Nina and David's six-year-old son
Maggie: lives at 75, Moreland Road; had a holiday in Chile
Xavier: Maggie's boyfriend; lives in Chile
Belen: Maggie's friend
Sam Davies: lives at 56, Moreland Road; works on a newspaper
Hannah: Sam's wife
Emma, Alicia: Sam and Hannah's daughters

Places in the story

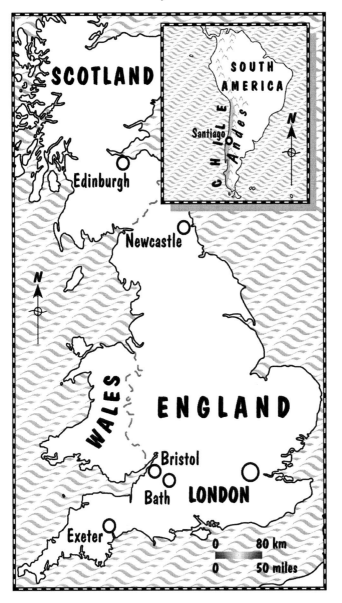

Introduction

Moreland Road is a street in the city of Bath, England.

One Friday evening in March, at six o'clock, people were coming home from work as usual. The schoolchildren were already at home.

A woman's voice was coming from number 12. 'Jason, are you doing your homework? You've got to do it before you go out to see Maria tonight.' But there was no answer. Jason was listening to music and couldn't hear his mum.

At number 48 David Sen wasn't home yet, but his wife was. Thirty-two-year-old Nina Sen was tired after a long week of work at the bank. She had some news for her husband, but she wasn't sure how to tell him.

Across the street was number 75. Maggie was in the living room, sitting on the sofa. She was thinking about something. It was a nice something, because she had a smile on her face.

And then there was Sam Davies, from number 56. He was walking slowly home, looking a bit worried. Actually, he always looked worried. Money was his problem. He never had enough for everything. How was he going to tell his wife that they couldn't have a holiday this year?

So, just another ordinary Friday …

Chapter 1 *Jason's future*

'Jason! Did you hear me? Are you working?' Jason's mum heard nothing from his room. She decided to go and see what was happening.

She stood outside the door of his bedroom for a minute and then she walked in. Jason was sitting on the floor and looking at some photos.

'What are you doing, Jason?' she asked.

Jason turned off his music and looked up.

'Do you remember this?' He gave her a photo. 'It's me when I was five, and Maria. She was really pretty – well, she still is. It was my birthday party, wasn't it?'

'Yes, I think so,' his mum said.

'It was the last birthday before Dad left,' Jason said. 'I remember it very well.'

'The party, or the day Dad left?' asked his mum.

'Both,' said Jason. 'In my mind, they both happened on the same day.'

'They didn't, but it all happened a long time ago,' his mum replied. She walked to the window so Jason couldn't see her face.

Simon, her husband, left their house in Moreland Road early one morning twelve years ago. He wrote her a letter and put it on the kitchen table. And then he left. For twelve years she didn't hear from him. No letters, no birthday cards for Jason. Then, last week, there was a phone call. 'Why did you go?' she asked Simon again and again. He wanted to meet her. 'No,' she said, but she wanted to say yes.

Jason's mum turned away from the window. 'Jason, what about your homework?' she said. 'Why are you looking at old photos?'

'I want to find all the ones I've got of Maria. I want to take them with me to London, you know, when I go to art school.' He smiled at a funny photo of Maria, aged eleven.

'It's a bit early to think about all that, Jason,' his mum said. 'You're not going until the autumn. And you don't know if you're going to get a place at the art school.'

'I will, I'm sure I will. When I went to visit them two weeks ago they said, "We think your work's very good. We really like your ideas."'

'I know, but … anyway, where are you going with Maria tonight?' asked his mum.

'Broad Street Bar. There's a great reggae band on,' said Jason.

'Have you told her about going away to art school in September?' asked his mum.

'Yeah. She's fine about it, I think,' he replied. 'I can come home at the weekends.'

'You won't …' his mother began and then stopped.

'I know what you're thinking,' said Jason. 'But we're different. We'll always be together.'

His mother left the room and went downstairs. 'Maybe Jason and Maria are different,' she thought. 'They've known each other since they started primary school. But I thought Simon and I were different, and look what happened.'

'Mum.' Jason came into the kitchen. 'I'm going round to Maria's now. I'll have something to eat at her house. OK?'

'Have you finished your work?' asked his mum.

'Yes. Stop asking me. See you later – about twelve. OK?' And Jason left the house before his mum had time to say anything else.

Five minutes later the phone rang. Jason's mum jumped out of her chair, looked at the phone and thought 'Simon.' She answered it. 'Hello,' she said in a very quiet voice.

'Oh, hi, Mrs Campbell. Is Jason there?'

'Maria!' Jason's mum almost shouted her name. 'No, sorry, he's left. He's on his way to your house.'

'Oh no!' said Maria.

'Is there a problem?' Jason's mum asked.

'No … Yes, I can't go out with him tonight. But it's OK, I'll tell him when he arrives here,' answered Maria. 'Bye.'

Jason's mum sat down. She drank a little red wine. She thought about the phone call from Maria. She thought that Maria's voice was a bit strange. She hoped nothing was wrong.

Chapter 2 *Nina's new job*

Nina Sen's work at the bank was over for the week. She was at home at 48, Moreland Road with her six-year-old son, Max. He was eating sausages and chips.

'I got 100% in maths today,' he said.

'Did you? That's great!' Nina answered. 'You're good with numbers – just like me.'

'Is Dad at work?' asked Max.

'Yes, but he'll be home soon. He's got the evening off,' Nina replied. David Sen worked as the top cook at Julie's, an expensive French restaurant. He worked long hours and very often he didn't get home until late.

'Oh good! Mum, can my friend Adam come to football with us tomorrow?' asked Max.

'Of course he can. Do you want to watch a bit of TV after dinner?' Nina wanted some time to think before David came home.

But she didn't get much time, because ten minutes later she heard David come in.

'Hi, Nina.' David kissed her. 'Where's Max?'

'Watching TV,' said Nina. 'How was the restaurant today?'

'Good. You know Dan?' asked David. 'The new assistant in the kitchen? Well, one of my cooks was ill today so Dan did some cooking. And he was great. He has a French grandmother and he can remember some of the food she made. So he's got lots of ideas for the new menu.'

'Daddy, Daddy!' Max shouted, running into the room.

'Hello, tiger,' said David. 'Let's go and read a story, and then you can tell me all about your day.'

Father and son left the kitchen. Nina could hear Max's excited voice. He was really happy to see his father.

'I'm lucky,' thought Nina. 'Why do I want to change things?'

She cooked dinner for herself and David.

'Are you ready to eat?' asked Nina when David came back to the kitchen. 'There's something I want to talk to you about.'

'Mmm. I'm not sure I like the sound of that. Is it something important?' he asked.

'The director from head office came to the bank today. He told me I was the manager of the month,' Nina said.

'Well done! Does that mean you'll get more money?' David laughed.

'In a way, yes. He asked me to be the manager in Newcastle. That's a really big bank, about five times the size of the one here.' Nina stopped and looked at David's face. 'So yes, more money.'

'Ah,' was David's only answer. Then a few seconds later, 'And what did you say?'

'I said I was interested,' Nina answered. 'I also said I wanted to talk to you. What do you think?'

'First thought,' said David, who stood up to get a glass of water, 'well done you. You work hard and I'm pleased for you. Second thought – what about my job? Third thought – Newcastle is so far away from here.'

'I thought all that too,' said Nina. She went across the kitchen and stood with her arms around David.

'And what about Max? He loves his school and his friends. And there's my mum and dad to think about,' continued David. 'I know they live in Exeter, but it's only a hundred kilometres from Bath and we see them quite often.'

'They could come with us. I'm sure they'll be happy in Newcastle. Your mum was born near there, wasn't she?' Nina was trying to think of some more good reasons. She really wanted this new job.

'Yes, but they have all their friends around them now, and they love living in Exeter,' David answered. 'It's a big thing to move at their age.'

'Forget them for a minute. What about you?' asked Nina.

'Well, you know I love working at Julie's,' David replied. 'We've got a good name since that newspaper wrote about us. It's an exciting time, and I don't really want to leave. Of course, I'm sorry the restaurant isn't mine, but we haven't got the money to buy it, so …'

'I really want to say yes, David,' Nina said. 'I think this is just the beginning. Maybe I could become manager for a big area in a few years and after that … well, who knows? Then we could buy two restaurants and …'

'Slow down,' said David with a smile. 'We haven't decided yet. When does the job start?'

'In three months,' replied Nina. 'David, we're still young. It could be exciting to start again in a new city.'

'True,' replied David slowly. 'When do you have to give the bank an answer?'

'Well, they want me to decide by the beginning of next week,' Nina said.

'Say yes, then,' said David quickly.

'What?' Nina looked at David. She couldn't believe it.

'Well, we can't buy Julie's – that's what I'd really like,' David answered. 'But I can get another job in a good restaurant in Newcastle. And your work is important. I know you love it.'

'Oh, David, you're wonderful. I'm so pleased I married you!' Nina laughed. 'I'm going to write to head office and tell them before you change your mind.'

David pulled Nina close and kissed her. 'I hope we've done the right thing,' he said. 'Anyway, now I'm going to have a long hot bath and think about it. And then I must phone Mum and Dad – I haven't spoken to them all week.'

'Don't tell them yet about Newcastle,' said Nina. 'Let's keep it to ourselves for the weekend.'

Nina sat at the table and wrote. Then she walked down Moreland Road with her letter and put it in the post box on the corner. She heard a soft 'plop' sound as it fell onto the other letters in the box. 'We've decided what to do and nothing can change that now,' she thought.

Chapter 3 *Dinner at Maggie's*

Maggie was sitting on the sofa. She had a photo in her hand. She was thinking about her holiday in Chile last month. She and her friend Belen went to Chile for three weeks, walking in the Andes mountains. It was a wonderful time. 'Well, actually, I don't think the holiday was as wonderful for Belen as it was for me,' Maggie thought. She looked at the photo and saw a happy group of young people.

They looked happy because the day's walking was finished. They were also happy because that was the day they saw the beautiful bird. A condor, the famous bird of the Andes, flew high above them in the sky that day and stayed with them for hours. Maggie was sad to see it fly away at the end of the day.

'It was a very important bird for the Inca people, you know,' said Xavier, their group leader. 'On lots of old Inca buildings you can see an unusual cross. It's unusual because it has three levels. Like this.' And Xavier drew the cross on the ground.

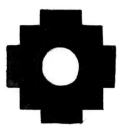

He continued, 'For the Incas, each level was a different world – the lower world, this world and the higher world. And there was an animal for each world. The higher world had the condor. So you see, these birds were very special, very important for the Inca people.'

The group were interested in Xavier's stories. Belen was more interested in Xavier. From day one Maggie knew that Belen liked Xavier. Well, he was great-looking and friendly with everyone. Belen talked to Maggie a lot about Xavier. What he said to her, how she felt. 'This is exactly what she was like when we were at school together,' thought Maggie. 'I hope I don't have to listen to this all holiday.'

At the end of the first week, Maggie went for a walk after dinner without the others. She didn't go far. She just wanted to be quiet and on her own with the stars in the dark sky. She stood looking up and then she knew that someone was behind her. She turned round and saw Xavier.

'Are you OK, Maggie?' he asked.

'Fine,' she replied. 'It's beautiful here, isn't it? I love the mountains. It's so different from where I come from.'

'I was born near here, so I love it too,' Xavier said.

They sat and talked for a long time. She learnt about his life and about the life of ordinary people in Chile.

From that day, she and Xavier had a special friendship. They often talked together after dinner, and something more than a friendship began. And of course Belen saw it.

'It's OK, Maggie, really,' said Belen. 'I don't mind.' But Maggie felt she *did* mind, and sometimes she saw Belen looking at her rather coldly.

But at the end of the holiday things were OK between the two friends. And Belen actually said she wanted to go on holiday with Maggie again.

Maggie got up slowly from the sofa. She enjoyed dreaming about her time in Chile, but she had to make dinner. Belen was coming tonight. She walked into the kitchen and started cooking the meat for the lasagne.

'Oh, I forgot to buy the tomatoes,' she thought. She took her money and left the house. She walked quickly to the shop at the end of her street.

In her house the phone rang and, of course, nobody answered it. Then the answerphone started: 'Hi, this is Maggie. Sorry, I'm not here to take your call but please leave your name and number, and I'll call you back later. Thanks.'

There was a small noise at the other end of the phone – someone was getting ready to speak. But the person didn't leave a message or their name and number.

Maggie came back with the tomatoes. She saw the message light on the phone. 'Probably Belen,' she thought. 'Maybe she's going to be late.'

Maggie played the message, but there was nothing to listen to.

'Strange,' she thought.

She went into the kitchen and finished the lasagne. Then she took a glass of red wine into the living room. She picked up the phone. 'Telephone number 07788 536782 called today at 1900 hours,' she heard.

Maggie wrote the number down and thought, 'I don't know anyone with that mobile number.'

But then she heard someone at the front door. It was Belen.

'Hi, Maggie,' said Belen and gave her a kiss. 'Mmm, something smells good.'

They walked into the living room and Maggie gave Belen a glass of wine.

'It's good to see you,' said Maggie. 'You look great. I love your hair.'

'Thanks. And how's the lovely Xavier?' asked Belen. 'Have you heard from him?'

'Yeah, I have,' said Maggie. 'I got an email last week. He was in an Internet café in Santiago.'

'Great! I thought it was just a holiday romance. But I'm really pleased for you … No, really I am,' said Belen quickly when she saw Maggie looking carefully at her.

'He says he's coming to England very soon – maybe next week,' said Maggie.

'Really! So soon? It must be love!' said Belen with a smile.

'Well, I don't know about that.' Maggie laughed. 'He doesn't say anything about love. Just that he's coming and that he's written me a letter to tell me everything.'

'Everything about what?' Belen asked.

'I don't know. It's a bit of a strange email. Look, you can read it.' Maggie gave the email to Belen. She read:

Hi condor-girl

I'm coming to England very soon. I need to get away from Chile for a bit. Have written to tell you everything. Can't say much now. Looking forward to seeing you a lot.

Much love

Xavier

Chapter 4 *Sam has money problems*

Sam arrived at his house, number 56. The lights were on in every room, and he could see his sixteen-year-old daughter, Emma, sitting at her computer in her bedroom.

Sam went inside the house and put his bag down. 'Wonderful,' he thought. 'No more work until Monday.' Sam worked for the town's newspaper – the *Bath Chronicle*. He was a reporter, but not a very important one. He quite liked his job, but he didn't get a lot of money for it. When he started work at the newspaper twenty years ago, he had big ideas. He wanted to work there for a few years, and then move to London to work for one of the big newspapers. But time moved on and he didn't.

Sam still wrote about the ordinary lives of people in Bath and sometimes … sometimes a big story. Then all the people on the paper had to work together and it felt good again – for a short time.

'Hannah, where are you?' called Sam.

'Upstairs with Alicia,' a voice replied.

Sam went upstairs and found his wife, Hannah, in the bathroom. Two-year-old Alicia was playing in the bath with about ten yellow plastic ducks.

'Hello, my favourite two girls,' said Sam and kissed them both.

'I heard that, Dad,' called Emma from her bedroom. 'What about me? I thought I was your favourite.'

'That was yesterday – when you made me a cup of tea,' said Sam and walked into his older daughter's room. Emma was looking at something on the Internet.

'I'm trying to find something about Chile for my geography teacher,' said Emma and turned to give her father a kiss.

'Go and ask Maggie. She's just come back from Chile,' replied her father.

'No, it's OK. I'll find it on the Internet. It's quicker.

Anyway, she probably doesn't know much about the Mapuche Indians. Dad, you know I really like geography, don't you?' asked Emma.

'Yes,' replied her father.

'Well, our teacher wants to take us to Norway after school finishes in the summer. She told us about it today. It sounds wonderful. Can I go?' Emma looked at her father. He could see how excited she was.

'It'll be expensive, won't it?' asked Sam.

'I'm not sure,' replied Emma, but she knew it wasn't cheap. 'There's the money I got for my birthday. We can use that.'

'Yes, but that's not enough for a holiday to Norway. I'll talk to your mum about it,' said Sam, and he left the room – again thinking about money.

Sam went into his other daughter's bedroom. Hannah was sitting on the bed. Alicia was nearly asleep so Sam kissed her goodnight.

'How much does Emma need for Norway?' he asked Hannah as they walked downstairs.

'A lot – about £700, I think. And she has to tell her teacher on Monday if she's going,' replied Hannah. 'She really wants to, Sam.'

'I know. I'll try to find the money from somewhere.' Sam walked into the back garden for a cigarette. Hannah sat down at the kitchen table to read the newspaper.

Hannah looked up when Sam came back in and said, 'I could get a job, Sam. But I really want to stay at home with Alicia for a bit longer.'

'I know, and that's fine,' said Sam. 'I'll ask Jeremy to lend us some money. I don't like doing it, but I've done it before.'

His older brother, Jeremy, had a good job. He worked in the world of computers where nobody thought about not having enough money. Jeremy was strong – some people thought he was hard, not strong. Every job he got was better than the last one. He wasn't happy if life was too quiet and easy. He was a doer, not a thinker. His wife was the same. They both worked and played really hard. 'It's good that they don't have any children because there isn't enough time for them in their lives,' thought Sam. Jeremy didn't understand how expensive children were. And Sam hated asking his brother for money. He could tell that Jeremy felt sorry for his younger brother.

'Why don't you get a better job, Sam?' Jeremy always asked. 'You're intelligent, you could do anything.'

'I like my job,' replied Sam. 'I don't want to work anywhere else.' That wasn't really true, but he could never let Jeremy know that.

And this was the same conversation Sam and Jeremy had on the phone that Friday evening. But then it changed …

'I'm sorry, Sam, but I'm not going to lend you the money,' said Jeremy.

'Pardon?' said Sam.

'No, no money this time. You need to think about your job. Get a job with more money. You've got to change, Sam. Every time you need money, you come to me. Well, I think it's too easy.' Jeremy stopped.

Sam put the phone down. His head was hurting. He couldn't believe it. His own brother didn't want to help him. His own brother talked to him like that, and made him feel small and dirty.

Sam went back into the kitchen.

'What did he say?' asked Hannah.

'Fine,' said Sam. 'He'll lend us the money, so Emma can go to Norway.'

'I know it's difficult for you to ask, so thank you, my love,' said Hannah and kissed him. Sam didn't look at Hannah and went to find Emma.

Chapter 5 *Jason and Maria*

Maria opened the front door of her house and let Jason in.

'Hi,' said Jason and kissed Maria. She took his head in her hands and looked at him for a few seconds.

'What are you looking at? Have I got something on my face?' asked Jason, and he kissed her again.

'No, I just wanted to look at you – you've got a lovely face,' replied Maria and walked into the living room.

'Are you OK?' asked Jason, following her. 'I haven't seen much of you this week.'

'I'm fine,' replied Maria. Then she turned and looked at Jason. She saw someone who was her best friend. She saw a person she loved, but she knew that she was going to change everything.

'Jason, sit down. I need to talk to you,' said Maria. She took his hand. 'There isn't an easy way to say this, but I've met someone else.'

'What do you mean – met someone else?' For a moment Jason didn't understand. Then his face went white.

'When I was on holiday with my family in France at New Year I met a man and …' (this was the difficult bit to say) 'and I think I love him.'

'You said you love me,' said Jason in a loud voice.

'I did. I do. I do love you, but maybe like a brother. I feel a different love for François.' Maria looked at Jason. 'Oh Jason, I'm sorry. I didn't want this to happen.'

'You don't love him,' said Jason. 'It was just a holiday romance. How can you fall in love with someone else? Have you heard from him since the holiday? Have you seen him? Does he say that he loves you?'

'Yes, he loves me too,' Maria answered. 'We've emailed each other every day, and he came to London last week for a few days. I saw him then when I stayed at my sister's.'

'You told me your sister wanted to spend some time with you,' said Jason. 'So that wasn't true, was it?'

Jason looked at Maria. He couldn't believe what was happening.

'When we finish school in the summer, I'm going to Paris to study. François is studying there at the moment,' Maria said, not looking at Jason.

'You've thought of everything, haven't you? When did you decide all this?' Jason asked.

Maria didn't reply.

Jason got up, put on his coat and said, 'I'm going. I can't stay here. It hurts just to look at you.'

'Will you be all right?' asked Maria.

'I don't know. And anyway it's not your problem now, is it?' replied Jason angrily.

'Jason, please don't,' said Maria. 'Don't go. We need to talk some more.' But Jason was already running out of the front door.

He ran and ran until he couldn't run any more. He wasn't angry any more, but just so sad. He started to walk slowly home. He hoped his mother was out – he didn't want to talk to anyone.

When he got to his house, he saw the lights were on. He tried to open the door quietly, but he couldn't.

'Is that you, Jason?' called his mother from the living room.

'Yes,' he replied.

She came to the door of the living room. 'Why are you back so early?'

'I'll tell you tomorrow,' replied Jason. 'I'm going to my room now.'

'Please can you come into the living room for a moment,' his mother said.

'Do I have to?' asked Jason.

'Yes,' his mother replied.

Jason followed his mother into the living room and saw a man sitting on the sofa.

'Jason,' said his mother. 'This is your father, Simon.'

Jason looked at the man and said nothing. Simon said nothing, but couldn't look at Jason. After a minute or two Jason said coldly, 'So where have you been for the last twelve years?'

His father replied, 'It's difficult, but let me try and tell you what happened.'

But Jason didn't want to hear any more things that evening. For the second time that day he ran out of a house. He went to the river and sat looking at the water. He felt lost. Everything was different. Maria loved someone else. A strange man – someone he called 'Dad' twelve years ago – was sitting in his house. Jason felt he was going mad.

The weather was cold and it was raining, but he just sat looking at the river. For a moment he thought about jumping into the water and letting it take him away. 'Who will be sorry? Nobody,' he thought. But, deep inside, he didn't really believe that.

He put his hand into his pocket and found some cigarettes. He lit one, stood up and turned away from the river. For hours he walked the streets of Bath. The rain was still falling and he was wet through. At about three o'clock in the morning he was outside the city's mail depot. There was a lot happening. Big vans were arriving with bags of letters. Jason was happy to stand outside the gate and watch the bags going into the building. He stopped thinking about his problems for a bit and time passed. One of the men shouted to him, 'Hey mate, you all right? Want a job or something?' Jason didn't answer.

A voice called out from inside the building, 'Harry, tea's ready. Leave those bags and come and get it.'

The big gate opened to let the next van in. And Jason just followed. The man at the gate didn't see him behind the van – he was too busy reading his newspaper. The driver got out of the van and went inside. Then there was nobody but Jason. He wanted to get out of the rain, so he got into the van and sat down between the bags of letters. It was dry and comfortable. He smoked his last cigarette and then closed his eyes.

He woke up a short time later when he heard the sound of people laughing in the building. For a moment he didn't know where he was. Then he remembered. He knew he must go home and talk to his mother. Then there was his father. Jason was angry with him, but he did want to know why he was back. 'And I don't want anyone to find me in this van,' he thought. He jumped out and waited in the dark for the gate to open again. When it did, he ran out.

A voice called out behind him, 'Hey, you! Stop!' But he didn't. He ran on. His head was hurting and his clothes felt wet and uncomfortable.

There was only one thing in his life that made him feel good – going away to art school in the autumn. It was really important that he heard from the London art school soon.

Chapter 6 *Nina and David talk*

David lay in the bath. He thought about Nina's new job, and about all of them moving to Newcastle. He loved working at Julie's and he was sorry to leave it. And Max liked his school. But Nina was important too. David knew she was wonderful at her job.

He got out of the bath and put on his jeans and a blue sweater. He went into Max's bedroom. His son was asleep. David sat on his bed for a few minutes. Then he gave him a kiss, turned off the light and left the room.

'Just going to phone Mum and Dad,' David called to Nina.

'OK. Remember, don't tell them about my new job,' said Nina.

'No, I won't,' replied David.

David phoned his father.

'Hi, Dad. Are you OK?'

'Fine,' replied his father. 'Your mother and I had a lovely walk by the sea this afternoon. Anyway, it's good you phoned. We wanted to tell you there's something in the post for you. For your birthday on Tuesday. It'll be a surprise, I know, but I hope it's a good surprise.'

'That sounds interesting,' said David. 'Are you going to tell me anything more about it?'

'No, you'll have to wait. Let me just get your mother. I know she wants to speak to you,' his father said.

'Joan!' his father shouted to his mother. 'It's David on the phone.'

'Coming.' David heard his mother's voice. And then he heard her say in a quiet voice to his father, 'Have you told him?' and the answer, 'No.'

'Hello, David,' said his mother. 'Are we going to see you soon? Can you come down next weekend?'

'Yes, on Sunday,' said David. 'We can't on Saturday because I'm working, but Sunday will be fine.'

'Oh good,' replied his mother happily. 'We want to see our lovely grandson again. We're lucky that you live near so we can see him quite often.'

David said something, but all the time he was thinking, 'How can we tell them that we're taking him away to Newcastle?'

'I'll give the phone back to your father now. I know he wants to tell you something about the garden,' his mother said. 'See you all next Sunday.'

'Bye, Mum,' David said. He then listened to his father talking about some ideas he had for his garden. David could hear how excited he was. His father was only really happy when he was outside and doing things.

At the end of the conversation his father said again, 'I hope our surprise for your birthday is what you want.'

'I'll ring you as soon as I get it,' replied David. 'Bye for now, Dad.'

David put the phone down and walked into the living room.

'Everything OK?' asked Nina.

'Yes, fine,' said David. 'I said we'll go down to see them next Sunday for the day. That's OK, isn't it?'

'Sure.' Nina saw the look on David's face.

'Mum said how she loved having Max so near,' said David, 'and I felt bad. They're getting older and they'll be so sad when we tell them about Newcastle.'

'Oh, David, I know, but they'll want us to do the right thing for us – as a family,' replied Nina.

'But now I really don't know if it is the right thing any more,' said David quietly.

They talked for hours and the questions were always the same: 'Is it right for us to go to Newcastle?' 'Do we ask your parents to go with us?' 'Do we forget about the new job and stay in Bath?' And then there was a new idea: maybe David and Max could stay in Bath and Nina could go to Newcastle for the week and come home every weekend. But how could David look after Max and work in the restaurant?

In the end they agreed. It was the same as their earlier decision. Newcastle in June for all the family.

'It'll be OK, won't it?' asked Nina.

'I hope so, love,' replied David. 'I really hope so.'

Chapter 7 *Maggie's visitor*

Belen gave Xavier's email back to Maggie.

'That's very strange,' she said. 'Maybe he's done something wrong – perhaps the police are after him or something.'

'No, not Xavier,' said Maggie.

'Why not, Maggie?' answered Belen. 'I mean, we were only in Chile for three weeks. How well do we know him? Have you had any other emails or letters from him?'

'Yes, an earlier email, but it didn't say anything about coming to England,' replied Maggie.

'Oh well, there's nothing you can do – just wait for the letter and hope it's nothing bad,' said Belen.

'I've just remembered something. Do you mind if I make a quick call?' asked Maggie. 'Someone phoned me just before you arrived, but they didn't leave a message.'

'Go ahead,' said Belen. 'I'll go into the kitchen.'

'No, no problem,' answered Maggie. 'Stay. I won't be a minute. Then we can eat.'

Maggie rang the mobile number.

'Hello,' said a foreign voice. It was a man.

'Oh hello,' said Maggie. 'You called this number earlier – Bath 726549. Who are you?'

'I'm sorry,' answered the man. 'It was a wrong number.'

'Oh, OK. Bye then,' said Maggie and put the phone down.

'Wrong number.' Maggie turned to Belen. 'Someone with a Spanish-sounding voice, I think.'

'From Chile, perhaps?' asked Belen.

'Maybe,' said Maggie. 'Anyway, it's not important. Let's go into the kitchen and have dinner.'

Maggie and Belen ate the lasagne. They looked at photos from their holiday and laughed at some of the things they remembered.

There was a noise from the living room and they both jumped.

'It's OK.' Maggie laughed. 'It's only the window. When it's windy, it always makes a noise.'

But then there was another, different noise. Someone was at the front door.

'What a bad time to call,' said Maggie.

She walked to the front door. When she opened it, she saw a man.

'Yes?' she asked. 'Can I help you?'

'Are you Maggie Cox?' asked the man.

'Yes,' answered Maggie. 'And who ...' But she didn't finish her question.

The man came into the house and closed the door behind him.

'Excuse me!' said Maggie angrily. 'What are you doing? Who are you?'

Belen heard her shouting and came out of the kitchen.

'Sit down, both of you,' said the man quietly. 'I don't want to hurt you.'

Belen and Maggie sat together on the sofa.

'I'm looking for a friend of yours – Xavier Santos,' said the man.

'He's not here,' said Maggie and Belen at the same time.

'Who are you?' asked Maggie.

'Let's just say I'm a friend of the Santos family,' answered the man. 'I know he's in England, and I want to talk to him.'

'I haven't heard from him since we got back from Chile,' said Maggie quickly.

'Really?' said the man. He walked round the room and looked at everything – postcards from friends on holiday, the phone bill that was on top of the TV. Then Maggie remembered Xavier's email – it was on the table next to her. It was too late to move it. The man saw it.

'So this is from another Xavier, is it? Where's the letter he talks about in the email?' asked the man.

'I haven't had it yet,' said Maggie. She was afraid and she could feel Belen was too. She didn't understand what the man was doing in her house.

'How did you know where I live?' asked Maggie.

'I found your address in Xavier's home,' said the man. 'And your photo. Did you have a good time in my country, Maggie?'

Maggie didn't answer the question. She asked, but half of her didn't want to know, 'Why are you looking for Xavier?'

'He's got something that I want,' said the man. 'But maybe he gave it to you to bring back to England.' The man walked up to Maggie and stood very close.

'He didn't give me anything,' said Maggie.

'Maybe he didn't, but I know that Xavier will come here soon. And when he does, I'll be ready for him.' The man looked hard at Maggie. 'You did a bad thing, Maggie, when you chose Xavier,' said the man. 'He's not right for a nice girl like you.' He moved away. 'Remember, Maggie, I'll come back.'

Belen and Maggie jumped up when the man left. 'You must phone the police, Maggie,' said Belen. 'This is terrible. You must come home with me. You're not safe here.'

Maggie phoned and told the police everything. She told them, 'I'm not going to stay here. I'm going to stay with a friend tonight. You can call me on my mobile, 04776 567831.' The police asked her to go to the police station the next day.

Maggie put some things in a bag, ready to leave with Belen.

'I'm so stupid,' said Maggie. 'I thought Xavier was really nice. I believed he loved me, but he was just playing.'

Maggie and Belen called a taxi and left Moreland Road half an hour later.

Chapter 8 *What Sam didn't know*

'How am I going to find £700?' thought Sam that Friday evening. 'And why didn't I tell Hannah about Jeremy?'

But it was too late now. Emma was going to Norway. 'That's so great, Dad! Thank you,' she said and kissed him. It made Sam happy to see her so excited.

'I know what I'll do,' thought Sam sadly. 'On Monday morning I'll take some of the jewellery my mother gave me before she died. There's a jeweller's shop on the way to work. I'm sure they'll be interested in buying diamond rings.' Sam didn't want to sell the jewellery. He knew his mother wanted Emma to have it.

'Maybe my brother is right,' he thought. 'I do need a job with better money. I don't know how much longer we can go on like this.'

* * *

That Friday morning, six hundred kilometres away in the city of Edinburgh, something important happened that could change Sam's life. But Sam knew nothing about it.

Two people, a man and a woman, arrived at the offices of lawyers Barrett, Grabbe and Lennox.

A man took the two visitors upstairs to the office of Frank Barrett. It was a very old-fashioned place with big, dark wood furniture. There were hundreds of law books all around the room.

'Good morning,' said Mr Barrett to the visitors. 'It's Paul and Sonia Cooper, isn't it? Please sit down.'

'Thank you,' said Sonia and sat down next to her brother, Paul.

'I'm sorry about your father,' said Mr Barrett. 'We looked after his business for years here.'

'Thank you,' said Paul. 'He was ninety-one when he died. But now we need to know what he decided to do with his money and things.'

'Paul!' said Sonia. 'That sounds terrible!'

'It's OK,' said Mr Barrett. 'Let me tell you what he wrote in his will.' Mr Barrett didn't always enjoy reading a will to a family. Sometimes there were surprises in it that they didn't like.

'I leave my house and all that is in the house to my two children, Paul and Sonia. My money I give to my grandchildren, Robert, Amy and Charlie.'

Paul and Sonia looked pleased. He continued, 'But not all of it.' Their smiles became smaller.

'I want to leave some of my money to a special person who was a good friend to me in my life – Samuel Davies.

'About thirty years ago, when my wife died, Sam lived next door to me. He was a young man, but he spent many

40

hours with me at that time. He visited me most days and listened to me when I talked about my wife. He was a true friend. I have never forgotten how kind he was. I want to say thank you to him and to give him £50,000.'

A few minutes later, Mr Barrett finished reading and the office was quiet. Then Paul Cooper said, 'Samuel Davies is a lucky man – £50,000 is a lot of money, just for talking to Dad.'

And Sonia said, 'I don't remember him. Well, that's what Dad wanted to do, and it's his money, so that's that. We can't change anything. But how much will there be for the grandchildren – Paul's children?'

'I'm not sure yet. We'll have to wait and see,' said Mr Barrett. 'We have to let Samuel Davies know. It could take quite a long time – you know, the address your father gave us could be wrong now. But I'll write to you as soon as I know.'

'But if you don't find him, what happens to the money?' asked Sonia.

'Oh, I'm sure we'll find him. It could take months, but we usually find people in the end,' replied Mr Barrett.

Paul and Sonia left the lawyer's office quietly. Mr Barrett gave some papers to his secretary and she wrote a letter to Samuel Davies. At lunchtime she took the letter to the post office. As she put it in the post box, she thought, 'Lucky Samuel Davies. What's he going to do with £50,000?'

* * *

Back in Bath that Friday evening, of course Sam had no idea about Mr Cooper and his money. He went to bed unhappy. Was it right to sell his mother's jewellery? And what job could a man his age get that paid more money?

Chapter 9   *Fire!*

At three-thirty on the morning of Saturday 15th March, a small fire started in a van at the back of the mail depot in Bath. Nobody saw it at first because everyone was inside the building.

Then someone smelled something and shouted, 'Fire!' Another person ran outside and saw what was happening. Someone else phoned the fire service. They tried to put out the fire, but they couldn't.

The fire service arrived very quickly and put out the fire. But two big bags of letters were lost. In those bags were four very important letters for some people in Moreland Road.

St Martin's School of Art
Charing Cross Road
London W1 8XA

Jason Campbell
12 Moreland Road
Bath BA6 5LZ

13th March

Dear Jason

Thank you for coming to see us last week. We really like your work and we think that you are the kind of student who will do well here at our college.

We are very happy to offer you a place here from September. As you know, there are many students who want to come to this art school. So it is important that you reply to us. Please tick (√) the box below and return the letter to the above address by 25th March.

We look forward to hearing from you soon.

Yours sincerely

Neil Parker

Neil Parker (Course Tutor)

....

☐ Yes, I can take a place on the art course, starting in September.

☐ No, I cannot take a place on the art course, starting in September.

120 Wharf Road
Exeter

13th March

Dear David

First of all, Happy Birthday! We hope you have a
really lovely day.

We've been thinking about our future and we want
to do something with our money. We have enough for
ourselves, so we've decided to spend some. We know
how hard you work at Julie's and we know that you've
always wanted it to be yours. So we've bought it for
you. We met Jean-Pierre last month and agreed a
price. Yesterday we heard that it's now ours - well,
yours actually.

We both know that you're going to make the
restaurant better than ever. Can we come to
dinner on your first big night?

Lots of love to our wonderful son
Mum and Dad

Santiago, 6th March

Dear Maggie

Hope you got my email. And I hope this letter won't make you angry.

I'm coming to England because I must leave Chile. I haven't done anything wrong, but my brother has. He's in with some bad people. My brother has disappeared - nobody knows where he is. His 'friends' think I've got some of his papers, but I haven't. So I want to come to England and get away from all these problems. Maybe I can get a job and stay there for a bit.

Also I want to see you. I think we're at the beginning of an exciting time together.

I'll be with you very soon. Until then please believe me that I HAVE DONE NOTHING WRONG. Please email me and tell me I can come.

lots of love and kisses
Xavier

Barrett, Grabbe and Lennox
34 Queen Street
Edinburgh EH2 3XJ

Samuel Davies
56 Moreland Street
Bath
BA6 5LX

14th March

Dear Mr Davies

We are writing about Mr Thomas Cooper, who has
sadly died. Mr Cooper has remembered you in his
will and we would be grateful if you could write to
this office as soon as possible.

Yours sincerely

Frank Barrett

Frank Barrett

Conclusion

And what happened to Jason, David and Nina, Maggie and the Davies family?

* * *

Jason went away for two weeks to stay with his grandmother. She looked after him and he began to feel better about himself. When he got back to Bath he was sad that there was still no letter from the art school in London. He phoned the school, but it was too late. The school said he could have a place the next year. For a year, Jason stayed in Bath and did lots of different jobs. Simon, his father, came to the house sometimes and Jason began, slowly and carefully, to get to know him.

* * *

Nina's letter to the head office of the bank arrived safely. David never got the letter from his parents, but his mum and dad phoned him on his birthday and he learnt about the restaurant. It was the best birthday present in the world. Nina decided to work in Newcastle and come home at the weekends. They were lucky because David's niece came to study at Bath University. She stayed with them and looked after Max. But it wasn't easy for the family. David wanted Nina to come home and work with him in the restaurant, but she stayed at the bank in Newcastle for eighteen months. Then she took the job of area manager in Bristol – a city twenty-five kilometres from Bath.

* * *

Maggie never heard from the Chilean visitor again. She never heard from Xavier again either, and he never arrived in England. Maggie was very sad. She really thought that she and Xavier were great together. It was hard for her. She wanted to believe that he was a good person, but all her friends told her to forget him. Sometimes she thought about going back to Chile to find him. But in the end, she didn't. She decided that probably it was just a holiday romance for him after all.

* * *

Sam sold his mother's jewellery and gave Emma the money. After a few days, he had another conversation with his brother. Then he decided to leave his job at the newspaper and write a book. He worked at home so he could look after Alicia too. At first, it was strange for him, but slowly he began to enjoy his new life. It was exciting to write and Alicia was an easy child. Hannah got a good job in a shop, which she enjoyed. They were still short of money, but one day about three months later he got a letter from Barrett, Grabbe and Lennox. Life began to look a lot better for Sam and his family.